THE BATTLE *of* NEW ORLEANS

D1554148

THE BATTLE *of* NEW ORLEANS

Plantation Houses *on the* Battlefield *of* New Orleans

SAMUEL WILSON, JR.

A Louisiana Landmarks Society Book

PELICAN PUBLISHING COMPANY
GRETNA 2011

Copyright © 1989, 1996 by Louisiana Landmarks Society
All rights reserved

Published by arrangement with the Louisiana Landmarks Society by
    Pelican Publishing Company, Inc., 2011

First printing, 1989
Second printing, 1996
First Pelican edition, 2011

---

*The word "Pelican" and the depiction of a pelican
are trademarks of Pelican Publishing Company, Inc.,
and are registered in the U.S. Patent and Trademark Office.*

ISBN 9781589809963

Printed in the United States of America
Published by Pelican Publishing Company, Inc.
1000 Burmaster Street, Gretna, Louisiana 70053

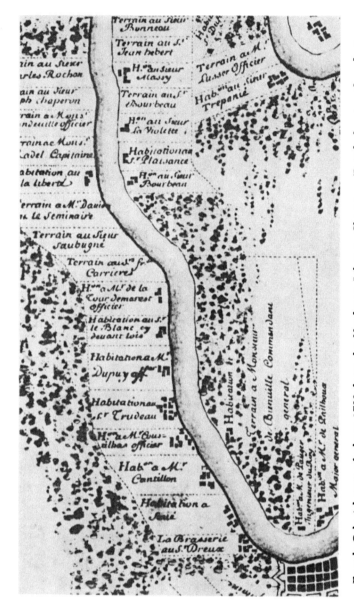

French Colonial map of about 1723 from the Newberry Library, Chicago. Detail showing the plantations below New Orleans.

2

I. INTRODUCTION

The land over which the British campaign against New Orleans in 1814-1815 was waged was one of rich plantations that had been cultivated from the earliest days of the French Colony.

The area in the early days of settlement was known as Pointe St. Antoine, deriving its name from a bend in the river of that designation.

According to the maps of the various engagements fought between the British and Americans in the final major struggle of the War of 1812 — maps prepared by Major A. Lacarriere Latour, Andrew Jackson's principal engineer—the activities of the rival armies extended over a distance of about six miles on the East Bank of the Mississippi River. The "seat of war" extended from the up-river plantation of François Balthazar Languille to the down-river plantation of Charles Jumonville de Villiers and included the plantations of Edmond Macarty, Jean Rodriguez, Antoine Bienvenu, Ignace de Lino de Chalmet, Pierre Robin Lacoste, Pierre Denis de La Ronde, and Jacques Phillippe Villere.

The battlefield of New Orleans has always been a point of interest to visitors to New Orleans. The English traveler and feminist, Harriet Martineau, who visited New Orleans barely 20 years after the battle, wrote interestingly of it in her *Retrospect of Western Travel* (Vol. II, page 155), published in 1838.

"We were taken to the Battle-ground, the native soil of General Jackson's political growth," wrote Miss Martineau. ". . . My delight was in the drive to it, with the Mississippi on the right hand, and on the left gardens of roses which bewildered the imagination. I really believed at the time that I saw more roses that morning than during the whole course of my life before."

She considered this experience "a precious luxury" because "gardens are so rare in America." She deplored the red brick, galleryless villa built by an Englishman as "obstinately inappropriate to the scene and climate." Continuing, Miss Martineau said:

> All the rest were an entertainment to the eye as they stood, white and cool, amidst . . . flowering magnolias, and their blossoming alleys, hedges and thickets of roses. In returning we alighted at one of these delicious retreats, and wandered about, losing each other among the thorns, the ceringas, and the wilderness of shrubs. We met in a grotto, under the summer-house, cool with its greenish light, and veiled at its entrance with a tracery of creepers. There we lingered, amidst singing or silent dreaming. There seemed to be too little that was real about the place for ordinary voices to be heard speaking about ordinary things.

Of all the important plantation houses which stood on the battlefield at the beginning of the campaign of 1814-1815, none has survived, but Harriet Martineau saw practically all of them on her visit to the Battleground in the 1830's. Only a few ruins still stand to mark the site of the Pierre Denis de La Ronde house. All the others have disappeared completely. Each had had an interesting

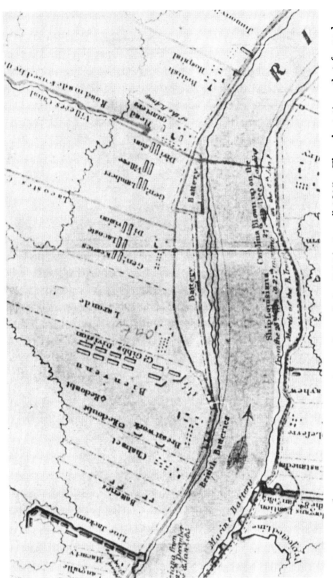

Detail from Latour's "Map Showing the Landing of the British Army" 1815. The plantations that formed the battlefield, from Languille's down as far as Jumonville's are shown.

history, and several were of considerable architectural importance.

A map dating from approximately 1723 in the Newberry Library in Chicago shows the several plantations located in the area at that time. These were, in order descending the river: "Plantation of the Sieur LeBlanc, formerly Law"; "Plantation of Mr. de la Tour Demarest, officer"; "Land granted to the Carriere Brothers"; "Land granted to the Sieur Saubugne"; and "Land granted to M. Davion and the Seminary." Approximate identification of the early plantations with those at the time of the Battle of New Orleans can be made. Father Davion's land became the Lacoste plantation, after having been granted to the Ursuline Nuns in 1727, from whom Lacoste derived his titles. The land next above, Sanbugne's, was later granted to the French military engineer, Adrien de Pauger, and ultimately became the plantation of Pierre Denis de La Ronde. The Carriere brothers' land was later granted to the Royal Attorney-General Fleuriau from whom Antoine Bienvenu derived his titles. The plantation of de la Tour Demarest was probably that of Ignace de Lino de Chalmet. Those farther up river, including perhaps the Rodriguez and Macarty plantations and several other small ones, probably derived from the LeBlanc plantation. Inasmuch as the boundary lines did not remain constant, over the decades, there may therefore, be considerable overlapping of property.

Another interesting French Colonial map, dated 1 March, 1753, shows all the concessions from New Orleans to English Turn. The Ursuline Nuns are

Detail from Col. Alexander Dickson's "Sketch of the Position of the British and American Forces during the Operations against New Orleans from the 23rd Dec'r, 1814, to 8th Jan'y 1815."—Courtesy of the Royal Artillery Institution.

shown in possession of the area later Lacoste's and part of de La Ronde's, M. de Mazan owning the rest. The plantation shown as belonging to Messrs. Derneville and de Reggio on this 1753 map became Bienvenu's. The next belonging to M. Mandeville in 1753, became Chalmet's. Part of the 1753 plantation of Messrs. Henry and LeSassier is probably also included in the Chalmet plantation. The next two plantations were those of de La Tour and M. Maret. They were probably heirs of M. de La Tour Demarest whose name appeared on the earlier map mentioned.

II. LANGUILLE'S PLANTATION

The battlefield plantation nearest to New Orleans was that of François Balthazar Languille, a native of Paris, who purchased the plantation in 1803 and 1804 from the succession of Antoine Bienvenu. It is difficult to trace the exact succession of titles because of frequent exchange of properties among the same people.

Today, this plantation is now part of the property of the American Sugar Refinery and it contained until June, 1965, when it was torn down, the intersting old colonnaded house known as Three Oaks.

According to Lacarriere Latour, Languille's house served as headquarters for Captain Peter V. Ogden's company of Orleans Dragoons, while at its rear the command of General John Adair was drawn up on the night of January 7, 1815, the eve of Sir Edward M. Packenham's fatal assault on Andrew Jackson's Rodriguez Canal line.

No description of Languille's house has survived, but it is obvious that Three Oaks could not have existed as early as 1815 in its present form, a style not found in Louisiana until at least a decade later. It is possible, however, that some of the original walls may have survived and been utilized in a new house.

In the *American State Papers* (Vol. 2, Public Lands, p. 316) Languille's claim is stated as follows:

> No. 185. Francois B. Languille claims a tract of land situated in the County of Orleans, containing eight arpents and nine toises in front (about 1600 feet), the upper line adjoins lands of Delery Desilet . . . the lower line, adjoining lands of Philip Laneau . . .

This claim was confirmed by the Federal Government to a depth of 40 arpents, the usually accepted depth of all Mississippi River plantations in the colonial period, unless a second concession of additional depth had been specifically granted by the Spanish authorities. Languille also claimed such a second concession, but this claim was denied. The *American State Papers* (Vol. 2, p. 345) record that:

> The claimant (Languille) states that Antoine Bienvenu, from whom he purchased, obtained a grant from the French Government, in 1754, for this back depth, together with a larger quantity; but he not having produced any evidence of such grant, and it not appearing in the records of the book of grants, we therefore reject the claim.

An old map in the Paris archives, dated March 1753, shows that this was then the plantation of the "Sr. Bienvenue", and an old, partially burned page from what was probably such a book of grants, now in the Tulane University Library, records the

9

Three Oaks Plantation House, belonging to the American Sugar Refining Co., built about 1831 by Sylvain Peyroux, possibly incorporating parts of the walls of the house of Samuel B. Davis that stood here in 1815.

. . . concession to the Sr. Bienvenu of the land that might be found - - - beyond the - - - of the 40 arpents.

To Monsieur de Kerlerec (chevalier of the Royal and) Military Order of St. Louis, Captain of the Vessels (of His Very Christian Majesty), Governor of the Province of Louisiana, and

Monsieur D'Auberville, Intendant (Comissaire Ordonnateur) in the said Province - - - Humbly represents Antoine Bienvenu, that he finds himself - - - with the plantation that he bought from M. de Vaudreuil - - - (which is) why he prays you to grant him - - - adjoining the said land (of) eleven arpents in width by forty (in depth), all this (additional) depth as far as Lake Borgne, if it - - -.

at New Orleans, 3 August 1753
signed Bienvenu.

Unfortunately much of this interesting document has been destroyed or is illegible. It does indicate, however, that this was formerly the plantation of the Marquis de Vaudreuil who succeeded Bienville as governor of the province in 1741. After his arrival in Louisiana Vaudreuil bought a plantation from Bienville on the West Bank of the river, but soon found it not to his liking, as he wrote to his brother on March 1, 1744:

I never could have done anything with Mr. de Bienville's Plantation; besides the badness of the ground, we run the risk of losing our negroes by often crossing the river. . . .

On November 21, 1743, therefore, an act of sale was passed at the Government House in New Orleans, whereby the "High and Mighty Lord Messire Pierre de Rigaut de Vaudreuil," Governor, purchased from Jean François Gauthreau, General Guardian of the King's warehouse in New Orleans, a plantation of ten arpents, seventeen toises and two feet front on the river and the usual forty arpents in depth, plus the unconceded lands extending back to the lake, located below the city between the plantations of the Sieurs de Gauvrit

11

and Dalcour, all in accordance with a survey prepared by Ignace François Broutin, engineer-in-chief of Louisiana. The purchase price for this plantation with its buildings, negroes, cattle, etc., was 30,000 livres.

With this purchase Vaudreuil was greatly pleased and wrote of it to an associate in Canada on March 1, 1744:

> . . . I have made (the purchase) of a plantation which costs me 30,000 liv. to be paid in four years, on which there are 34 strong well-made negroes, all manner of buildings, and even a fine dove-house flock'd with about 100 pigeons, 57 oxen and cows, as many sheep, and the rest in proportion. There are 180 arpents of grubb'd up, tilled land ploughed and sowed; I have built, with bricks, ten vats to make indigo, and hope the produce of four years will pay the principal. Provisions being dear occasioned my buying this plantation, and if you live in this place you must have one; besides, I had it almost for nothing. I was offered, before I laid out anything upon it, 15,000 Liv. more than I am to give. I think I have made a good bargain.

Documents of the French Superior Council, in the Louisiana State Museum, record the installation of Kerlerec in place of Vaudreuil on February 6, 1753, and on April 16, these same records contain an inventory of the plantation that Bienvenu had bought from Vaudreuil and apparently leased back to him temporarily until his departure. The furnishings of the main house are listed by rooms in this most interesting record of an important French Colonial plantation.

After Languille acquired his eight arpent plantation he apparently subdivided it into several smaller properties. Part of it, 200 feet by 1000 feet, was sold by him on November 16, 1805, to Joseph McNeil who owned it at the time of the

Battle of New Orleans. He sold it on November 17, 1815, less than a year after the battle, to Alexander Jackson.

Joseph McNeil, a member of the first vestry of Christ Church, rented the house to the Reverend Philander Chase, a young New Hampshire clergyman. Because of his wife's failing health from tuberculosis, Rev. Chase accepted the appointment to become the first Protestant rector in New Orleans in 1805, seeking a milder climate for her sake. While living in the McNeil house, the young rector established in it a school, because, he wrote. "a school (was) much needed among the Protestants." So successful was this venture, "down the river about three miles" (*La. Hist. Quart.*, Vol. 22, P. 143), that Rev. Chase moved it into town.

The property just below McNeil's had been sold by Languille in November, 1805, to William Kenner, who purchased it for John Clay, brother of Henry Clay. The next year Clay sold it to Dr. Robert Dow, a good friend of the Rev. Chase and later a member of the vestry of Christ Church.

On the upper side of McNeil's, Languille sold another 200 foot by 1000 foot tract on August 2, 1805, to William Harper and Samuel R. Davis. Two years later, Davis bought Harper's interest in the property. Davis, a protege of Daniel Clark, was a young sea captain who managed Clark's rope walk. He became Captain of the Port of New Orleans, and finally took Clark's daughter, Myra, to live in his home, rearing her almost as his own. As Myra Clark Gaines, she became the famous New Orleans litigant. In 1813, Davis went north

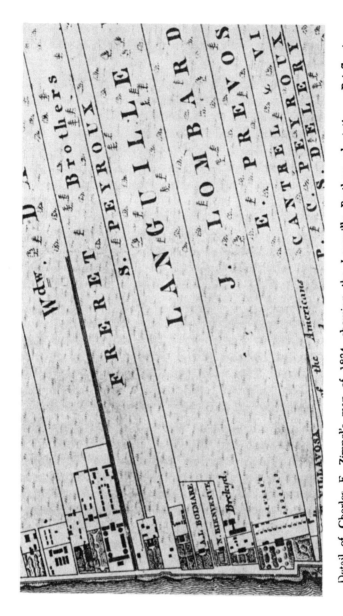

Detail of Charles F. Zimpel's map of 1834, showing the Languille Brothers plantation. Briefly in 1805 Languille's plantation had also included the adjacent lands here shown as S. Peyroux and Freret Brothers.

14

and participated in military action in Delaware. When New Orleans was threatened in 1814, he was ordered to proceed there with his regiment, but arrived after the battle. He owned his house on the former Languille plantation until April, 1817, when, like McNeil, he also sold it to Alexander Jackson.

Both properties, plus another arpent above, were eventually acquired by Sylvain Peyroux who bought the former McNeil portion from A. L. Boismare on January 7, 1835, and the former Davis portion from Madame Jacques Kernion (Widow Guerin), on May 5, 1831, and the additional arpent above from the Freret brothers on May 30, 1836. When the Freret brothers bought the property together with the two adjacent arpents above, from Bernard Marigny on August 9, 1831, it was described as having on it a master house with surrounding gallery, kitchen, etc. This house, at the time of the Battle of New Orleans, was the property of George Deslondes. The one arpent property containing the house was sold by the Freret brothers to Pierre Darcantel on May 30, 1836, who then sold it to Frederick Roy on December 5 of the same year.

According to an interesting account published some years ago in a program for the St. Maurice Church Fair "The Roy property remained in the family until the New Orleans Terminal Company bought the property . . . The Roy homestead was early known as *La Maison a Jalousies*. It had belonged, during the War of 1812-15 to Mrs. Deslondes. . . . It was then a two story house. Frederick Roy remodelled it when he purchased it on his arrival from Bordeaux in the early 1830's, but still kept the blinds surrounding the galleries." Madame Deslondes had bought the property less than a year before the battle, on February 27, 1814, from Nicholas Roche. Roche had bought it from Laurent Sigur in 1809 who had in turn bought it from François Balthazar Languille on June 14, 1805.

When Charles F. Zimpel drew his notable map of New Orleans and its environs in 1834 he showed these various subdivisions of the former Languille plantation, each with its separate house and garden. The first two arpents above J. Lombard (the former Macarty plantation) were still owned by the Languille brothers, Jean François and Pierre Joseph, who inherited it from their father in 1828. In 1834 it contained a brickyard behind the house and garden. All this has long since disappeared and the site is now part of the Chalmette slip. Next above was the house and garden of N. Bienvenu, the 200 by 1000 foot tract that had been sold by Languille to William Kenner in 1805. Next came the country residence of A. L. Boismare, formerly owned by Joseph McNeil (and later sold to Sylvain Peyroux) also only 1000 feet in depth. The land behind these two properties still belonged to the Languille brothers. Next to Boismare was the 200 foot strip, to a depth of 80 arpents, also with a house and garden belonging to Sylvain Peyroux that he had bought from Madame Kernion in 1831. The house on this property is the one that has since become known as Three Oaks.

When Madame Peyroux died, the inventory of her estate made by the Notary L. T. Caire, listed this plantation and its several acquisitions and stated that Peyroux "has had the master house and its dependencies constructed." He probably did this soon after he bought the Kernion property in 1831 and when the house was finished, bought the properties on either side to give his new mansion a proper setting. The last private owners of

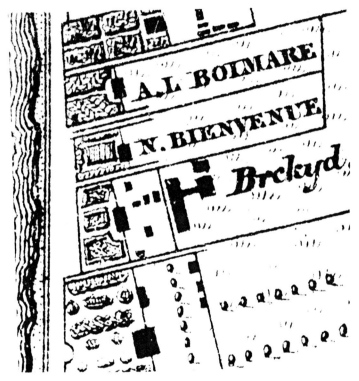

Detail from Zimpel's map of 1834 showing the Languille house and garden with the brickyard in the rear. The Macarty house, Jackson's headquarters is at the bottom. At the top is "Three Oaks," Sylvain Peyroux's house built in 1831. This plantation had belonged to Samuel B. Davis, guardian of Myra Clark Gaines in 1815. A. L. Boimare's had once been the home of the Rev. Philander Chase and N. Bienvenue's the home of Dr. Robert Dow.

this notable house were Mr. and Mrs. L. E. Cenas who for several years leased it from Eugene D. Saunders and then bought it from him in 1895.

The New Orleans Terminal Company early in this century, bought the house from Mrs. Cenas and sold it, as part of a large tract, to the American Sugar Refining Company in 1905. Unfortunately, the refinery demolished this fine old house after having maintained it in the public interest. The house was basically in its original form although fire damage many years ago required rebuilding the roof and probably the upper gallery and much of the interior trim. The floor plan consisted of four corner rooms without halls, and with two small rooms (or "cabinets") in the rear on either side of what was once a recessed porch, the whole surrounded by a two story Doric colonnade. The plans of both floors are similar and so like the typical earlier French type of house found in the Vieux Carré, as well as in the country, as to suggest that Peyroux built his house upon the foundations of the earlier house he had bought from Madame Kernion, and which had been owned by Samuel B. Davis at the time of the Battle of New Orleans.

III. EDMOND MACARTY'S PLANTATION

Immediately below Languille's plantation was that of Edmond Macarty. Of great architectural interest, and even greater historical importance, the master house of this plantation served as Andrew Jackson's headquarters during the Battle of New Orleans. This plantation of nearly four arpents frontage has had many changes of ownership. It belonged in June, 1790, to Espiritus Liotaud and

Augustus Faure, and later to Pierre Denis de La Ronde. After acquiring a larger and more important property a little farther down river, de La Ronde sold it on December 23, 1800, to Laurent Sigur, who at the time also owned the adjacent plantation which eventually became the property of de Lino de Chalmet. Sigur sold a small strip of the former de La Ronde property in 1802 to Nicolas Roche, and on January 5, 1804, disposed of the rest of it to Simon Ducourneau, who sold it the same day to Philip Lanaux. It was from Lanaux that Edmond Macarty bought it on February 17, 1807.

Some time after making this purchase, Macarty erected a new house upon it, probably intending to use it as a country residence. It is quite probable that his architect was the noted Jean Hyacinthe Laclotte, a native and resident of Bordeaux, who, at the age of 39 received his passport for "going to Louisiana to practice his art there."

The year Edmond Macarty purchased his plantation below the city, Laclotte made a very elaborate plan for the subdivision of the Faubourg Plaisance for Joseph Wiltz, the principal street of which eventually became Louisiana Avenue. Laclotte included in his drawing a plan for the development of a typical lot, showing the suggested plan of a country house with its surrounding gardens quite similar in character to those that surrounded Macarty's house. These gardens are most clearly shown on Laclotte's well-known print of the Battle of New Orleans.

The prominence that Laclotte gives to the Macarty house and gardens in his picture, its simi-

Detail from Laclotte's "Battle of New Orleans" showing the house

and gardens of the Edmond Macarty Plantation, Jackson's headquarters.

21

larity to Laclotte's plan of the Faubourg Plaisance, and its similarity to the Delord-Sarpy house (almost certainly designed by Laclotte in 1813 for Dr. Joseph Montegut) suggest that he was the architect for Edmond Macarty's country residence.

Unfortunately, Macarty did not long enjoy his fine new home, if indeed he ever lived in it at all. On November 13, 1814, he died, when scarcely thirty years of age. A little more than two weeks later Andrew Jackson arrived in New Orleans on December 2, 1814, and by Christmas day had taken over the Macarty house as his headquarters, using it until after the final victory on January 8, 1815.

It was not until March 1, 1815, when things began to return to normal after the battle, than an inventory was finally made of Edmond Macarty's estate. His widow, Marie Eleanore Destrehan, was then living in the new house of her father, Jean Noel Destrehan, in Conti Street — a house erected for him by the architect-builder William Brand in 1811. This house was elaborately furnished with all of Edmond Macarty's furniture, probably either removed from the plantation house before the threatened attack or following it. Or perhaps the Macartys were using the new Destrehan house on Conti Street while awaiting the completion of their own country residence. In any case, no furniture is listed in the plantation house, but only in Destrehan's.

The inventory, made by direction of the Probate Court, describes the country house as:

> A plantation situated at about one league and a quarter from New Orleans, below and on the same bank, having three arpents, twenty-six toises and five feet of front to

the river by eighty arpents of depth, bounded on one side by Mr. Amiant and on the other by Mr. Rodriguez, the establishments consisting in a new master house and some other buildings in very bad condition, the said plantation totally lacking fences (entourage) . . . $15,000.

The description of the buildings as "in very bad condition" and the total lack of fences probably indicates the damage resulting from the battle. Latour states in the *Historical Memoir* (p. 146): "All the pales of the fences in the vicinity were taken to line the parapet, and prevent the earth from falling into the canal." Latour also describes some of the damage inflicted by the British in their attack on January 8 (p. 158):

> The fire was at first very brisk, and was principally directed against Macarty's house, in hopes that the general and his staff might still be there. . . . The only mischief done by that prodigious expense of balls and shells, was that Major Chotard, assistant adjutant-general, received a contusion in his shoulder, and four or five pillars of the house were knocked down.

Major H. O. Tatum, topographical engineer, in his report of the campaign made to the Secretary of War (1. 156), refers to a British attack on January 1, 1815, in which:

> The firing (was) directed . . . at the house of Madame Mc Carthy (sic), occupied by the General as his headquarters. This building was considerably injured by the enemy's ball.

The historian, Alexander Walker, in his *Life of Andrew Jackson* (p. 134) says that:

> The planters' dwelling houses in 1814 were . . . (sometimes) in the chateau style like Bienvenu's and Macarte's, in front of the British camp, which consisted of two stories and an attic, the ground floor being usually paved with brick or marble, and the galleries supported by brick pillars, circling the whole building. These houses were surrounded by trees and shrubbery, so that, at a short distance, they could scarcely be seen. They looked to the

river, and were built usually at a distance of a few hundred yards from its bank, with cultivated gardens, or neatly trimmed lawns, shaded by spreading live oaks and pecan trees, and hedged around with a thick growth of orange and lemon trees, extending in front to the road, which follows the levee. The plantations were divided by slight but durable fences of cypress pickets. . .

Describing the action of December 28, Walker (p. 222) continues his remarks about the house:

Established in the fine old chateau of Macarte, which then, as now, could hardly be discerned at a short distance off, through the thick evergreen trees and shrubbery in which it is embowered, within one hundred or two hundred yards of the right of the entrenchments, Jackson kept an incessant watch over every movement of the enemy, viewing their camp through a large telescope, which an ingenious old Frenchman had loaned him for the occasion, and which was established in the dormer window of the chateau, looking down the river. This chateau still stands (1855), but little changed by the lapse of forty years. It has been the study and pride of its successive proprietors and occupants to preserve the premises, as much as possible, in the condition in which Jackson left them, after the war was over. Only such repairs as were absolutely necessary have been made. Even the cannon marks on the pavement, walls and pillars may now be seen, and the scarred oaks, cedars and pecan trees, which surround it, still bear the signs of strife that drenched with blood the fields around, that now smile with rural beauty and teem with agricultural wealth, and rendered the headquarters of the General-in-Chief the most exposed and insecure position of the whole camp. Hundreds of the cannon balls have been dug out of the garden, which were rained down on this favorite target of the British artillery.

After the battle and the settlement of her late husband's succession, the Widow Macarty resumed the cultivation of the plantation in association with her brother, Guy Noel Destrehan. This arrangement did not last long, for before the end of the year, she, too, had died. In her will, dated November 15, 1815, she expressed the desire that her brother continue the operation of the planta-

24

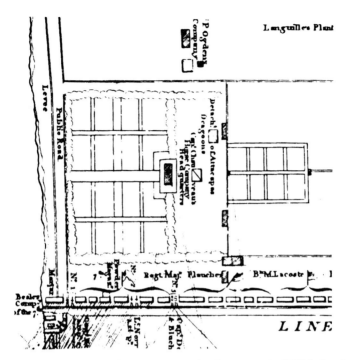

Detail from Latour's plan of the "Battle of January 8, 1815," showing the plan of the Macarty plantation and the adjacent Languille and Rodriguez plantations.

tion for the benefit of her two children. On December 21, the will was filed for probate, her father, Jean Noel Destrehan, being named tutor for the orphaned children.

The young son, Jean Edmond Macarty, died at the age of two on October 2, 1816. Accordingly, Destrehan considered it to be in the best interest of his surviving granddaughter, Myrtile, to dispose of the plantation. An auction was held on April 14, 1817, and on April 30, the act of sale to William W. Montgomery was passed before the notary, Michel de Armas.

The architect Latrobe, visiting the site with Vincent Nolte in 1819, made several sketches of the house and wrote an interesting description of it:

> Close to the river and separated only by the levee and road, is the old-fashioned, but otherwise handsome garden and house of Mr. Montgomery. The garden, which I think covers not less than 4 acres, is laid out in square walks and flower beds in the old French style. It is entirely enclosed by a thick hedge of orange trees, which have been suffered to run up to 15 or 16 feet high on the flanks and rear, but which are shorn down to the height of 4 or 5 feet along the road. The walks are bordered by very large myrtles cut into the shape of large hay cocks, about 8 feet high and as much in diameter. There are so many of them, and they are so exactly equal in size and form that the effect is curious if not elegant. The house itself is one of the usual French plantation houses of the first class, and I think by far the best kind of house for the climate, namely, a mansion surrounded entirely by a portico or gallery of two stories. The roof is enormous. However, in order to build the redoubt, the corner of the garden was cut off, and part of the orange hedge still grows, in a very decayed state, within the lines of the redoubt. The road has been turned round it. Mr. Montgomery intends restoring his garden to its former state, when the ruins of this work will entirely disappear.

Later, Vincent Nolte wrote: "The house was still standing in the year 1838, when I visited it and saw the cannon-balls still embedded in its walls, where the owners had, in their enthusiasm, caused them to be gilt, in the year 1822."

Alexander Walker visited the battlefield and described the scene as it was in 1855 (p. 307):

> The scene of these events has experienced slighter changes in the last forty years than the arena of any similar occurences in this land of change and progress. (The visitor) may take his position in the gallery of Macarte where

Jackson himself stood on the afternoon of the 7th January 1815 . . . Jackson's headquarters are nearly concealed by a luxuriant growth of the graceful cedars and cypress, — which here assume the most symmetrical proportions, tapering off into perfect cones and pyramids. A thick orange hedge almost excludes a glimpse into the handsome garden, where bloom all the flowers and shrubs of this rich soil and benignant clime. But the buildings stand as they did then, but slightly changed by the lapse of time. They are scarred in many places with marks of the severe cannonade to which they were exposed.

Ten years after the battle another event occurred that added to the historic significance of the Macarty plantation house. On April 10, 1825, the Marquis de Lafayette was received here as he approached New Orleans on his triumphal tour of the United States. An article published in 1889 (*La. Hist. Quart.*, Vol. 29, P. 313) by Edward C. Wharton, one-time editor of the *Picayune,* thus describes the scene:

". . . the Governor, the twelve marshals, and a brilliant military staff (proceeded) to the Battle Ground where Lafayette was to land.

About 11 A.M., a fleet of steamboats, crowded with spectators, . . . among them numerous ladies . . . came down from the City . . . Lafayette, (arriving on the steamboat Natchez) being told of this, at once went on deck, and, despite the pouring rain, stood there bareheaded, bowing to the applauding assemblage on the boats and the multitude, equally enthusiastic, on the levee.

At 2 P.M. the Natchez slowly approached the landing at the Battle Ground . . . and the Committee of Arrangements and Marshals received the General and his suite. They were at once conducted to an elegant landau, drawn by six white horses; and the whole party moved rapidly to the lofty and spacious mansion of Mr. Wm. Montgomery, which as the Macarty Plantation had been Gen. Jackson's headquarters in 1815.

The crowd of eager spectators that filled the broad galleries of the historic house, gave way in silence on the approach of the veteran, leaning on the arms of Messrs. Villere and Duplantier. Governor Johnson advanced to meet Lafayette . . ."

27

Speeches and responses filled most of the day and were fully reported in the *Louisiana Courier* for April 13, 1825. Late in the afternoon the ceremonies were concluded at the Macarty house and the march into the city began.

According to Zimpel's great map of March, 1834, the old Macarty property then belonged to J. Lombard. In 1861, Benson J. Lossing, in preparing his *Pictorial Field-Book of the War of 1812*, visited the site of the Battle of New Orleans and sketched the Macarty house as it then appeared (p. 1037). While he shows only one dormer window in the roof, the house actually had two as shown in Laclotte's print. Lossing's sketch, however, does show that the road was then located very close to the front of the house and the beautiful garden had disappeared, probably due to changes in the river bank, changes that eventually would envelop the site of this historic house.

Lossing mentions (p. 1039) that in the assault of January 1, 1815, "Jackson's headquarters at Macarty's was a special target. In the course of ten minutes more than a hundred balls, shells, and rockets struck the building, and compelled the commander-in-chief and his staff to evacuate it. The marks of that furious assault may be seen in all parts of the house to this day (1867)."

Lossing does not mention the name of the owner at that time but twelve years later, in 1879, John Dimitry, in the *Illustrated Visitors Guide to New Orleans*, says the property was then owned by Dr. M. F. Bonzano of the United States Mint.

The old home later became the residence of

The Edmond Macarty house, said to be from a daguerrotype made before the Civil War, in the collection of the late Stanley Clisby Arthur.

Henry L. Beauregard, son of Confederate General, P. G. T. Beauregard. His brother, René, lived a short distance below in a house that still bears his name, the house once used as the Visitors' Center for the Chalmette National Historical Park. It was during the Beauregard occupancy that the old Macarty house was destroyed by fire. In its issue of February 22, 1896, the *St. Bernard Voice* reported briefly that "the residence of Mr. Henry Beauregard burned down yesterday morning. A spark from the chimney set the old dwelling ablaze. It was insured for $4000." In its issue of the following Saturday, February 29, 1896, the Voice gave a more complete account of the fire, together with some of the history of the house, erroneously reporting, however, that it had been built by Montgomery:

When the Beauregard residence—one of the oldest landmarks of this section—was swept out of existence by fire last Friday, we were nearly ready to go to press, and consequently could not dwell at length on the sad occurrence.

It is very seldom that there is a fire in this parish, and consequently the cry of fire plunged everybody into a great state of excitement. . . . White and colored people, side by side, combatted the flames, but unfortunately, their labors were in vain. Fire engines were wanting, and without them the ancient residence must perish. . . . Mr. Henry I. Beauregard called at The Voice office on Saturday last, and requested us to express his sincere gratitude to all of those who so nobly assisted to fight the fire and save valuables. This building was erected just before the war of 1812 by William M. Montgomery, a wealthy merchant and planter. It was then considered one of the finest residences in the south, and as built then has stood the winters of nearly a century without any material alteration since the day it was built. Before the time when the war broke out there were many stories told of the great house, because of a jealous husband, who guarded his lovely wife in the strictest manner possible. Since that time the mansion and grounds have passed into many hands but the historic flavor which surrounded it has

The Macarty house from Benson J. Lossing's "Pictorial Field Book of the War of 1812," from a sketch made by Lossing in April, 1861.

never been obliterated, and even up to a day before it burned down there were visitors from the far north, who desired to be shown through the building. There have been many relics of the war of 1812 found in the yards around the house and Dr. Bonzano while repairing the building some years ago found imbedded in the walls and woodwork several rusty cannon balls evidently fired by the British artillery.

This fire was perhaps not the end of the historic house for it is said to have been rebuilt from the ruins only to be finally obliterated by the construction of the Chalmette Slip. *The Picayune Guide to New Orleans,* published in 1912 states that the house was torn down in 1907 to make room for the Frisco terminal freight sheds, as the Chalmette Slip was then called. This project was completed in 1908 but was then (1912) abandoned, partially silted-up and although costing about $4,000,000, had never been used. Eventually it did become, and still is, an important port facility. The site of the Macarty house is now covered by the river itself, the levee having been moved back when the slip was built.

Not a trace remains of what was perhaps the most significant house in the area of the Battle of New Orleans.

IV. THE RODRIGUEZ PLANTATION

Just below the Macarty plantation was a small property only half an arpent wide, facing the river and widening somewhat as it extended back toward the swamp. Along the lower boundary were the remnants of an old canal or mill race which General Andrew Jackson selected as the principal line of defense. It was known as the Rodriguez Canal, because this was the plantation of Jean Rodriguez, who bought it on September 29, 1808, from Daniel Clark, Louisiana's Territorial representative in Congress. Only a few months earlier, June 23, 1808, Clark had bought it from John Lynd who had acquired it from J. M. Pintard just two days before. Immediate owners before Pintard were Jean Baptiste Prevost, Jean Baptiste Drouillard, Nicolas Roche and Laurent Sigur.

Wood engraving of the Rodriguez house from a sketch by Knobloch, in Waldo's "Illustrated Visitors' Guide to New Orleans," 1879.

Rodriguez plantation buildings from Laclotte's "Battle of New Orleans." To the left are outbuildings of the Macarty plantation.

The buildings standing on the plantation at the time of the battle appear on Laclotte's print. These were probably built by Roche. The canal, or mill race, and the old mill that straddled it, were probably established between 1799 and 1802, when this was all part of the Sigur plantation. On the other hand they may have been built during the brief period in 1807 when this and most of the former Sigur plantation were owned by J. B. Prevost. The canal and the mill near the river appear on a survey made for Prevost on June 13, 1808, by the architect-engineer, Barthelemy Lafon.

The plantation house was built close to the line of the Macarty property and it was a small, raised structure erected on a fairly low brick basement. A gallery with chamfered wood columns extended across the narrow front and along the side facing down-river to the east. The western end of the front gallery was protected by louvered jalousies. The house was only one room in width with two semi-circular fan light French doors opening on to the front gallery. A single dormer overlooked the river from the double pitched, hipped, shingle roof. It was a typical small plantation house of the period.

Eventually, the Rodriguez house came to be confused with the Macarty house as being the one used by General Jackson as his headquarters. It may have been this confusion that caused the State of Louisiana to purchase it from Pierre Bachelot, February 19, 1854, for the site of the present monument.

The Rodriguez house was still standing when work was begun on the Chalmette monument,

Sketch of the battlefield made in 1819 by Benjamin H. B. Latrobe, showing the Rodriguez house on the right and the Macarty house on the left.

36

"Remains of Rodriguez's Canal" from a sketch made by Lossing in April, 1861. The partly finished monument is on the left.

designed by Newton Richards. The price agreed upon on June 28, 1855, was $59,000.

Either this sum was not made available or was insufficient, for when the shaft of the monument reached a height of about sixty feet the work was abandoned and the monument remained in an unfinished state until 1907 when Congress appropriated $25,000 for its completion. The design was changed to its present form and the structure was finally finished in 1908. By that time the Rodriguez house had probably disappeared. An excellent sketch of it appears in Waldo's *Illustrated Visitors' Guide to New Orleans,* published in 1879. John Dimitry, author of this portion of the text, says that "for years the house . . . now the shabbiest of ruins, has been known as the Jackson Headquarters." He states that the adjacent house, then owned by Dr. M. F. Bonzano, was the one used by Jackson.

The sketch engraved by Waldo and signed Knobeloch, on which the previously given description of the house is based, is somewhat at variance with the representation of the building on Laclotte's print. The latter shows the house with neither dormer window or side gallery, and shows close beside it a one story wing, possibly a kitchen, with a four columned porch across the front. The differences in these two drawings probably represent the changes made during the period of the Prevost ownership.

Latrobe, on visiting the battlefield in 1819 with Vincent Nolte, roughly sketched the arrangement of the buildings. Latrobe also made two rough pencil sketches of the battlefield in both of which the Macarty and Rodriguez houses are prominently shown. The more finished of these two sketches may have been intended as a study for a more complete water color painting to be done at leisure as Latrobe often did. He had applied a few washes to emphasize the shadows and had also indicated the materials of the Rodriguez house by notes and symbols, showing the roof as of shingles, the gallery as enclosed with "Venetian blinds" and an adjacent two story building on the Macarty property as of brick. Latrobe's sketch, made some three or four years after Laclotte's, shows that by this time the dormer window had been added (or Laclotte had merely neglected to show it), and that the front gallery had been enclosed with jalousies or "Venetian blinds" on the second floor. There is no side gallery and the adjacent small one story building is drawn much the same as it appears on Laclotte's print, the hole in the roof having, of course, been repaired by this time.

V. THE CHALMET PLANTATION

Down the river next to the Rodriguez property and canal was the largest of the several plantations comprising the field of the Battle of New Orleans. This was the plantation of Ignace de Lino de Chalmet whose name, which he always spelled without the final "te," has become synonymous with the battlefield itself.

The entire frontage of Chalmet's property was over twenty-two arpents (about 4400 feet), which he had acquired in two parts. The first, consisting of the lower six arpents, he purchased on February 9, 1805, from Charles Antoine de Reggio, who had bought it from Chalmet's aunt, the widow of Antoine Philippe de Marigny de Mandeville on July 13, 1794. These lands, originally ten arpents, had evidently been granted or purchased by Francois Philippe de Marigny sometime before his death in 1728. The following year, on September 26, 1729, his widow, Marie Madeleine Le Maire married Captain Ignace François Broutin, engineer-in-chief of the colony. Broutin was the architect of many notable buildings, the only one of which to survive being the old Ursuline Convent on Chartres Street. A daughter of this marriage became the mother of Ignace de Lino de Chalmet. After Broutin married the widow de Marigny, the plantation is referred to as his, but after their deaths it was inherited by her son, Antoine

Philippe de Marigny. Thus, except for the brief period between 1794 and 1805 when de Reggio owned it, this part of the Chalmet plantation has been in the continuous possession of this family since the earliest years of the French Colony.

The upper part of the property consisting of somewhat more than sixteen arpents adjacent to the Rodriguez plantation was not purchased by Chalmet until about a year and a half before the battle. He acquired it on June 14, 1813.

During the Spanish Colonial period, Pierre de Marigny de Mandeville purchased more than sixteen arpents of the old Marais grant next to his mother's property from Louis Boisdore and on February 16, 1798, gave it in exchange as part payment for the plantation of Laurent Sigur, a plantation that he subdivided in 1805 as the Faubourg Marigny.

On June 12, 1805, Laurent Sigur sold the plantation to Jean Baptiste Prevost, who sold it to William Brown, Collector of Customs for the United States at New Orleans. Evidently Brown invested in land beyond his capacity to pay, for on November 17, 1809, Governor W. C. C. Claiborne opened a letter he had written the previous day to Robert Smith, Secretary of State, to add this postscript:

> I have opened this letter to inform you, that William Brown the collector has ran off, and taken with him a large sum of public money. - I have by letter given the particulars to the Secretary of the Treasury: - I have sent in pursuit of this villain; but I fear he will not be overtaken.

As a result of this "infamy", Brown's property was seized and sold at auction on March 2, 1810. It

Ruins of Chalmet's plantation from Laclotte's "Battle of New Orleans."

41

was advertised in the *Louisiana Gazette* on March 6 as a "Sugar plantation . . . having seventeen and ¾ acres front by the usual depth, and about one hundred acres of Sugar Canes lately planted on the premises: the different buildings on said plantation consist of a large Dwelling House, Sugar Works, Store Houses, Saw Mill, Negro Cabins, and several other buildings, being bounded on one side by the lands of Mr. Ignatius Delino, and on the other by the property of Mr. John Rodriguez."

This sale was made for the benefit of Laurent Sigur's creditors, but the claim of the United States against Brown prevailed and the property was transferred to the Federal Government on March 15, 1811. Meanwhile, Philip Grymes, the United States Attorney, had negotiated for the sale of the property for $44,000 to Charles Mynn Thruston and his son-in-law, Henry Daingerfield. Thruston died in the principal house of the plantation and is said to have been buried "in a cluster of orange trees a short distance south east of the residence." On June 14, 1813, the property was sold to Ignace de Lino de Chalmet.

Chalmet probably took possession of the plantation house that Sigur had built but was then known as Brown's house. Unfortunately, no pictures or description of it are known. The act of sale merely mentions the buildings but gives no other information about them. The purchase price of $65,000 would, however, indicate that this was a well-developed plantation and the buildings must have been significant. Unfortunately, they were destroyed during the course of the battle and only their ruins appear on Laclotte's well-known print.

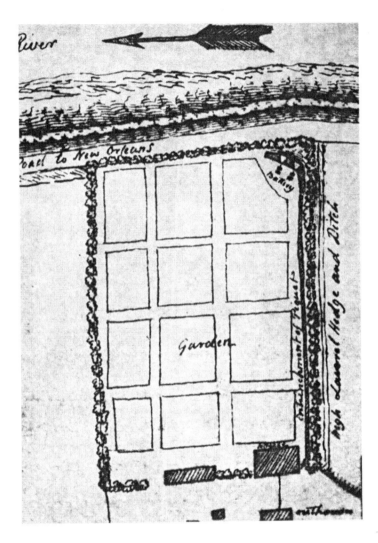

Sketch from British Colonel Alexander Dickson's "Journal of Operations," showing the arrangement of the house and gardens of Chalmet's lower, or original, plantation—Courtesy of the Royal Artillery Institution.

43

Chalmet's plantation was the area where the heaviest fighting took place in the engagement of January 8, 1815; the area which saw the greatest concentration of British troops and the area which contains the spot where General Pakenham fell, mortally wounded. Chalmet's plantation was occupied by the British on December 27, 1814, and, according to Latour, Jackson "ordered colonel Mackrea the commander of the artillery, to fire and blow up all the buildings on Chalmette's plantation, which lay within five or six hundred yards of our lines, as they protected the enemy from our artillery. This order was accordingly executed." The British subaltern Gleig describes the destruction vividly:

> The shrieks of the wounded . . . the crash of firelocks, and the fall of such as were killed, caused at first some little confusion; and what added to the panic was that from the houses beside which we stood, bright flames suddenly burst out. The Americans, expecting the attack, had filled them with combustibles for the purpose; and directing one or two guns against them, loaded with red-hot shot, in an instant set them on fire. The scene was altogether very sublime. A tremendous cannonade mowed down our ranks and deafened us with its roar; while two large chateaux and their out buildings, almost scorched us with the flames, and blinded us with the smoke which they emitted.

Major H. O. Tatum, Jackson's acting topographical engineer, in his journal refers to the buildings on Chalmet's plantation as "Brown's house." He states that on December 28, 1814:

> The enemy now formed their encampment in view of the line of defence. . . . This picquet occupied the grounds near the river from a distance of from 40 to 60 chains (4 to 6,000 feet) below the American line. They were covered from our view by enclosures of orange trees around the gardens at Brown's and Bienvenu's and a few lofty trees and some other undergrowths. In these gardens, etc., the picquets threw up works, under cover of which they secured themselves from the effect of our fire.

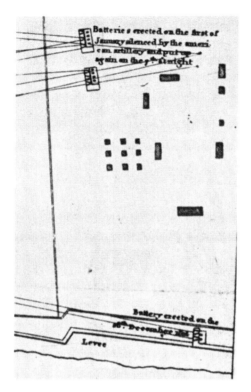

Plan of the arrangement of buildings on Chalmet's lower plantation from Latour's map of the "Battle of January 8, 1815."

Tatum, mentioning the American batteries erected on the West Bank of the river across from these plantations, declares that "furnaces for heating balls were erected . . . in order to destroy the houses on the left bank that incommoded our operations. Brown's house (Chalmet's) was soon destroyed by this means."

Alexander Dickson's "Journal of Operations" published in the *Louisiana Historical Quarterly* (July-Oct. 1961, Vol. 44, No. 3 & 4) contains several interesting sketch plans, one of which shows the locations of Chalmet's buildings and indicates that houses existed on both the original part of his plantation and the former Brown property that he bought later. One sketch shows the latter house with the batteries erected by the British behind it, noted, "house burnt 28 Dec." Between this and Bienvenu's another house is indicated labeled "Piquet House," undoubtedly the house of Chalmet's original plantation.

Another sketch in this important British journal shows a detailed plan of the arrangement of the out buildings and gardens around this latter house; indicating a large house with formal gardens in front surrounded by a "high laurel hedge". As Jackson had done at Macarty's, the British cut off a corner of the garden near the levee and erected a battery. Dickson, accompanying General Keane's troops up the river road on December 28, describes passing the Bienvenu plantation "and still further a house burning (about 3000 yards from the Enemies' great Picket house (Macarty's)) which the Enemy had set fire to as they retired." Here they were attacked and forced to retreat, for according to Dickson "the Enemies' fire had been so heavy, it was requisite to withdraw . . . to the right of the road, under cover of the ruins, Garden Hedges, etc. of the burning house." Within a week, and before the assault of January 8, 1815, both of Chalmet's fine plantation houses were destroyed.

Ignace de Lino de Chalmet was a member of an old and distinguished family. He was a posthumous son of François Xavier de Lino de Chal-

"Chalmette's Plantation," from a sketch made by Benson J. Lossing in April, 1861, "from the foot of the shaft of the unfinished monument, near Jackson's head-quarters and line of intrenchments."

met; born in 1755, and, at the time of the battle was just under sixty years of age. Chalmet's widowed mother later married Pierre Denis de La Ronde and their son, Pierre, Chalmet's half-brother, was the owner of another of the important battlefield plantations.

Chalmet, like many plantation owners, also had a house in New Orleans. His was a very small, simple cottage on Bourbon Street. His great-great-granddaughter, Mrs. Edwin X. de Verges, long interested in the Chalmette National Historical Park, says that "the family legend is that the elder Chalmette fought valiantly in the battle and escaped injury, and when the battle was won, he went to his town house, located on Bourbon Street between Bienville and Conti. Later, he rode back to the site of the battle, gazing sadly over the ruins of his plantation house and the land surrounding it. He felt then he was too old to start all over again, and he died Feb. 10, 1815, of a broken heart."

His widow, Victorie Vaugine, in filing the succession, declared:

> That all the furniture and papers belonging to the said succession, and which were located on the plantation where her said late husband dwelt, have been reduced to ashes by the fire which the American General judged necessary to have set to the principal house, and other establishments which were located on the said plantation; for the defence, of Louisiana against the English.

In 1817, two years after Chalmet's death, his entire plantation was sold to his half brother, Pierre Denis de La Ronde, who the same year sold it to Louis and Hilaire St. Amant, two free men of color. In 1832, the St. Amant brothers decided to sell off part of the property, the upper six and lower four arpents. In their advertisement of this sale, they stated that "On the six arpents of the upper part is found the line of defence of the American Army in 1815, and on the 4 arpents of the lower part are the four majestic Oaks where all those who come to visit the field of battle generally end their walk."

. . At this sale, the small tract in the upper part occupied by the René Beauregard House, once the Visitors" Center for the Chalmette Battlefield Park, was sold to Alexandre Baron who bought it for his mother-in-law, Mrs. Guillaume Malus. Here she built a house, and resided until her death in 1835. It then became the property of her son, François Malus, and her daughter, the widow of Alexandre Baron. The house had come to be known as the Baron house, and is so marked on Charles F. Zimpel's map of 1834. In 1848 Madame Baron donated her interest in the property to Lucien Malus, and in 1856, the place was sold to Caroline Fabre, widow of Michel Bernard Cantrelle. At that time, the house was probably a simple French-Louisiana type farm house, as modified then by newer American influences. The walls were of brick, painted red and "pencilled," that is, the mortar joints were painted with a white stripe, a common practice of the 1830's.

It is thus likely that Madame Cantrelle, after buying this, by then, old-fashioned house, had her granddaughter's husband, James Gallier, Jr., remodel it in more or less the form it now has. The Greek Revival brick columns could have been added at that time and the cornice raised to its present proportions to be in scale with them. This

René Beauregard house as it appeared about 1890. From an old photograph in the Cenas Collection of the Louisiana State Museum.

caused ·the pitch of the roof to be changed, resulting in the graceful curve around the lower part that has been so long admired. The fine interior staircase, the large slip-head window sash, the small pediment over the entrance door were all probably done at this time also. But the great columns. except for their plastered capitals and bases were only of brick, painted white, while the walls remained in their earlier painted state.

In 1866 Madame Cantrelle sold the house to Jose Antonio Fernandez y Lineros, sometimes known as the Marquis de Trava.

When the Marquis de Trava took possession in 1866 and named the house "Bueno Retiro", he probably also made some changes and, as his wife was also a relative of Gallier's it is likely that the alterations were again done by the same noted architect. The principal change was an addition at the west end, consisting of one room on each floor, each exactly the same depth as the rooms of the original house. This wing had a plaster cornice, a low parapet and a flat roof. The brick walls were then plastered and marked off or scored to resemble stone work. The pattern of this stone jointing extends also over the painted brick walls of the old house, indicating that all the plastering of the exterior walls was done at this time. Also at this time the upper rear gallery was enclosed in glazed casement windows with wood panels below them between the columns. An exterior wood stair was built at the end of this gallery alongside the new wing. Evidence of these various changes was found when the house was restored for the National Park Service in 1957.

Fernand Colomb house, probably built about 1832 when the St. Amant brothers subdivided the Chalmet plantation. Behind it were the four oaks mentioned in the advertisement of this sale. Demolished in the 1950's for the Kaiser Aluminum Co.'s plant.

When the restoration was begun, this 1866 wing had already disappeared, as had the exterior stair, and a later wing at the east end of the house, probably added in the 1890's. These elements were not reconstructed, nor was the rear gallery enclosure restored.

In 1880 the property was purchased by René Toutant Beauregard, son of the Confederate general, who owned it until 1904. It was then sold to the New Orleans Terminal Company which held it until 1948, when the State of Louisiana acquired it for incorporation into the Chalmette National Historical Park.

Near the center of the St. Amant property, and just above where they had had a canal dug in 1822, the United States National Cemetery was subsequently established. Land was purchased by the City of New Orleans on November 11, 1861, from Charles Rixner and additional adjacent land was bought in 1867. An interesting plan of Chalmette Cemetery was drawn by Louis Pilié in 1867 showing "Camp Chalmette fortifications," Confederate breastworks remaining from the Civil War. These were located on land now occupied by the Kaiser Aluminum Plant, as are also the four oak trees where Pakenham is supposed to have died. These oaks marked the lower end of the St. Amant plantation.

Nothing remains of the buildings that stood on Chalmet's plantation in 1815, nor of the structures built subsequently by various private owners. Only the René Beauregard house has survived.

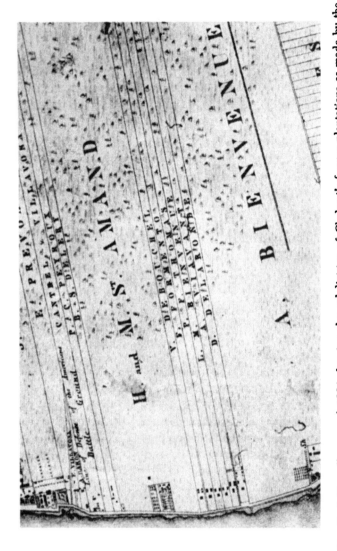

Detail of Zimpel's map of 1834 showing the subdivision of Chalmet's former plantations as made by the St. Amant brothers in 1832. The plantations included all the area between E. Prevost (Rodriguez in 1815) and A. Bienvenu.

VI. THE BIENVENU PLANTATION

Below Chalmet's plantation was the Bienvenu plantation. Lacarriere Latour does not give any detailed plans of Bienvenu's place as he did of the Macarty and de La Ronde properties. However, Bienvenu's property does appear on his general "Map Showing the British Army." The buildings seem to be located about in the center of the tract facing the river with breastworks and two British redoubts facing Chalmet's plantation and several batteries in front facing the river. Here General Gibbs' Division was located. Gibbs had taken this position on December 28, 1814. Bienvenu's buildings, while much closer to the river than de La Ronde's were, nevertheless, much farther back than Chalmet's. In the American bombardment from the west side of the river on January 4, 1815, Bienvenu's house was in the line of fire and some of its slave quarters were set ablaze.

Bienvenu's, at the time of the Battle of New Orleans, was one of the largest plantations in the area. It had been, and remained, in the same family ownership longer than any of the other properties in the vicinity. The earlier Bienvenu plantation had been located farther up the river in the French Colonial period. The first part of this later plantation — 14 arpents — had been purchased by Antoine Bienvenu from Madame Helène Fleuriau, widow of François Marie de Reggio on November 14, 1794. During that brief interval in 1803 when Louisiana was again under French domination. Bienvenu purchased an additional four arpents from his up-river neighbor, Charles Antoine de Reggio. The entire eighteen arpent plantation remained in the Bienvenu family until subdivided into 19 lots and offered for sale in 1843.

The lower ten of these nineteen lots and part of the adjacent de La Ronde plantation eventually came under a single ownership and was known as "Battle Ground Plantation" and so listed in the inventory of the estate of William Dunbar in 1861.

Perhaps the best description of the Bienvenu plantation and its numerous buildings is contained in the advertisement that appeared in the *Louisiana Courier* for October 15, 1831, after the death of Charlotte LaBarre, wife of Antoine Bienvenu, Sr.:

A Sugar Plantation situated in the Parish of St. Bernard about two leagues below the city of New Orleans, and on the same side of the river, measuring eighteen arpents fronting on the Mississippi, with all its depth extending to the Lake diminishing in width at forty arpents from the river of three arpents at the lower limit, and bounded above by the plantation of St. Amant brothers, and below by that of the heirs of Laronde.

The following Buildings are constructed on said plantation:

A two story brick dwelling house, divided into sixteen rooms or apartments surrounded by a spacious gallery; A brick sugar house, with two sets of kettles; A circular brick building, containing a steam engine, a sugar mill &c.

A brick curing house or purgery, calculated to contain one hundred and ninety-two hogsheads of sugar; One brick kitchen with front and back gallery. One brick store house; Thirty-three negro cabins; one brick Hospital; Pigeon house; Blacksmith shop; barn and other dependencies.

All the aforesaid buildings are in very good repair.

Zimpel's map of 1834 shows the Bienvenu plantation in some detail and on it the various buildings mentioned in the advertisement of 1831 may be distinguished. Almost exactly in the center of the tract and now quite close to the river, the principal house is set behind its formal gardens. The house with its gardens and accessory buildings are surrounded by fences which separate them from another fenced area containing the sugar house and the circular brick sugar mill with its steam engine and the curing house or purgery. These circular sugar mills were distinctive features of Louisiana sugar plantations, although very little seems to have been written about them. They were probably introduced into Louisiana about 1800.

Benson Earle Hall in his *Recollections of an Artillery Officer*, published in London in 1836, gives perhaps the best contemporary account of the Bienvenu house at the time of the battle. Hall visited it soon after he arrived with the British troops. He wrote (Vol. 1, p. 333):

> Close to the left of our line stood the house and plantation
> of Monsieur Bienvenu. It was an elegant mansion; much
> of the furniture had been removed, but enough remained
> to mark the taste of the proprietor. In the hall, which was
> floored with variegated marble, stood two magnificent
> globes, and a splendid orrery. One room contained a vast
> collection of valuable books. On entering a bed-room,
> lately occupied by a female of the family as was apparent
> by the arrangement of toilet &c, I found that our advance
> had interrupted the fair one in her study of natural his-
> tory, a volume of Buffon was lying open on her pillow;
> and it was evident that her particular attention had been
> directed to the domestic economy of the baboon and

57

monkey tribe, slips of paper marking the highly colored portraits of these charming subjects for a lady's contemplation.

Hall later returned to the house on January 1 to rest "on a heap of dried pea-straw in one of the outhouses." Here, he became engaged in an argument with one of his friends who soon after was killed in battle. The old friends had been reconciled before the one died of his wounds and, Hall relates (Vol. II, p. 5):

> We caused a grave to be dug near a group of beautiful trees in the garden attached to Bienvenu's house, and with humble but earnest prayers for his soul's welfare, consigned to the earth the mortal remains of poor Alic Ramsay.

Hall then continues, probably recalling the bombardment of January 4, 1815, writing that the Americans "wisely determined on drawing us out of the excellent cover afforded by the house of Monsieur Bienvenu, which he shortly rendered too hot to hold us." In a footnote, Hall adds:

> Finding that the destruction of this beautiful mansion was inevitable, I looked about to see if I could preserve anything useful, and fortunately discovered a heap of China plates half a dozen of which I carried off, without the slightest remorse of conscience. One of these, having escaped the fate of his fellows, I have still in my possession.

Major H. O. Tatum, in his journal also mentions the part played by the Bienvenu plantation in the events of the battle. He writes that, following the bombardment from the batteries across the river:

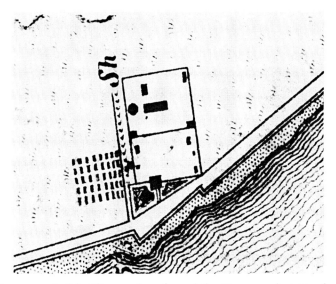

Arrangement of buildings and gardens of the Bienvenu plantation from Zimpel's map of 1834. The sugar house is in the rear, the Negro cabins to the left.

> The enemy had plundered Bienvenu's Sugar House of a number of hogsheads of sugar which were taken to the levee and converted into a battery from whence several shots were exchanged with our batteries on the right. The materials did not answer the end proposed, and the battery was silenced in a short time.

Alexander Walker in his *Life of Andrew Jackson* indicates that the Bienvenu house was one of the larger type and in somewhat the same style as Macarty's.

No pictures of the Bienvenu house have been found, but from the various descriptions, like Walker's and Hall's, it must have been one of the largest and finest in the area, and perhaps similar to the "Homeplace" at Hahnville, La., built, like Bienvenu's, in the 1790's, and one of the best examples of the French type of colonial plantation house. The buildings of Bienvenu's plantation have entirely disappeared and their site is now occupied by the Kaiser Aluminum Company, and other industrial operations. Whether or not the principal house was still standing when Walker visited the site and wrote his book in 1855 is not made clear.

VII. THE DE LA RONDE PLANTATION

Undoubtedly, the finest of the plantation houses on the field of the Battle of New Orleans, was that of Colonel Pierre Denis de La Ronde. A great house, said to have been built by de La Ronde in 1805, it much resembled in plan and detail the great French Colonial house built on the same plantation by a former owner, the Chevalier Balthazar Ponfrac de Mazan, in 1750.

It is the only house that stood on the battlefield in 1815 of which any physical remains have survived. Today a picturesque pile of red brick ruins stand on a small "island" formed when the St. Bernard highway was built to by-pass it on either side. The vine-covered, tree-shaded ruins are enclosed by an iron fence, and are always an object of great interest to the many tourists who visit the site, principally to admire the magnificent avenue of live oaks that stretches before it toward the river. The two rows of trees planted about a hundred feet apart, each contains about forty great trees spaced approximately fifty feet apart. This avenue belonged to the Southern Railway which maintained it for many years, though in the course of time several of the old trees have died and not been replaced, leaving gaps in the otherwise continuous leafy tunnel.

Various legends have grown up regarding the origin of this avenue of oaks, all crediting Pierre Denis de La Ronde with having planted them, but ascribing various dates to the planting. The usual story is that he planted them on his twenty-first birthday, April 20, 1782. This is most unlikely, as the property was, on that date, the plantation of Françoise Macarty, widow of Jean Baptiste Cesair Le Breton, who had bought it in 1774 and left it to her second husband, Maurice Conway, on her death in 1787. This eight arpent portion of the plantation passed through several owner-ships before it was purchased by de La Ronde on February 13, 1799, at auction of the estate of Joseph Connand. It is significant too that no mention is made of such an avenue of trees in any account of the Battle of New Orleans, nor does it appear on any of the maps of this campaign, including the rather detailed one by Latour that shows the arrangement of the gardens as they existed at that time. If this twenty-first birthday date ascribed for the planting is correct, it prob-ably referred to the birthday of de La Ronde's son of the same name, who was twenty-one years old on June 1, 1822, a much more likely date for the planting of the trees. One of the earliest representations of the avenue appears on Zimpel's map of 1834.

Latour's map of the engagement of December 23, 1814, fought principally on de La Ronde's plantation, shows the house fairly close to the old levee and closer to the river than is now the case. In front of the house, Latour shows a large formal garden divided by paths into twelve plots, the two center ones being additionally divided by diagonal

The de La Ronde mansion's facade facing the river. Photograph

by Mugnier, c. 1885, taken shortly before the building burned.

paths. The semi-circular form at the garden entrance is repeated by a similar semi-circular forecourt in front of the house. The nearly square garden is bordered by a hedge of trees, beginning at either side of the house and completely enclosing the area except for a central entrance way. The entrance drive from the river road did not lead to this gateway, but ran parallel to the upper side of the garden.

Latour explains that on the night of the 23rd, the American troops in this area "formed on a line almost perpendicular to the river, stretching from the levee to the garden of LaRonde's plantation and on its principal avenue." His drawing clearly shows this location, together with the successive positions of the British and American troops as the latter quickly drove the enemy back to Lacoste's neighboring plantation and finally back to Villere's. The British used de La Ronde's house until after the battle of January 8, using it principally as a hospital where their General Gibbs was to die and where General Pakenham's body was conveyed after his death in the field.

The house itself was one of the largest and finest of those referred to by A. W. Walker as "in the chateau style," but no documentary evidence that would establish the date of its construction has been found. The house and particularly its contents suffered considerable damage as a result of the Battle of New Orleans. Its use during that period is best described by the British officer, Benson Earle Hall, in his *Recollections of an Artillery Officer*. He wrote:

Long before daylight, on the morning of the ever memorable 8th I accompanied Colonel Dickson to the front; and after inspecting the various batteries, we took up our positions in the gallery of La Ronde's house, which commanded a tolerable view of the enemy's lines, and where we could also observe the result of our cannonade. Soon after our arrival, the batteries opened their fire, and our shots appeared to have effect. . . . The brave and much loved General Gibbs had been conveyed to La Ronde's morally wounded. With his dying breath he accused Colonel Mullins of having caused the ill-fortune of the day. . . . Colonel Dickson left me at La Ronde's to answer any inquiries made by officers of artillery, and to give any instructions required. The scene now presented at La Ronde's was one I shall never forget; almost every room was crowded with the wounded and dying. The bodies of two gallant generals (Pakenham and Gibbs) lay close to each other, and another (Keane) was severely hurt; mortifying defeat had again attended the British arms, and the loss in men and officers was frightfully disastrous. I was the unwilling spectator of numerous amputations; and on all sides nothing was heard but the piteous cries of my poor countrymen, undergoing various operations. The 93rd Regiment had suffered severely, and I cannot describe the strange and ghastly feelings created by seeing a basket nearly full of legs . . .

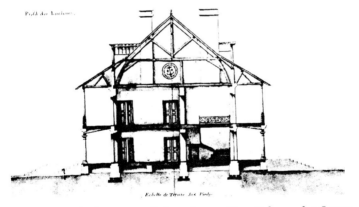

Cross-section of the proposed Intendance, New Orleans, by Ignace François Broutin, architect, August 23, 1749. One of the earliest architectural drawings showing a typical two-story Louisiana gallery.

(Ministère des Colonies, Paris)

De La Ronde himself describes the damages to his beautiful house in a petition he addressed to the U. S. Senate some months after the battle, seeking compensation for his losses. He presented also a certificate given to him by Andrew Jackson as evidence of his attention "to the public concerns on the invasion of the Enemy, to the detriment of his private one," but adding that the certificate "signed by the Savior of the state" was "more valuable to him as a testimonial of his conduct than as a voucher of his losses." Describing these losses, de La Ronde said:

> everything in the house or on the plantation that could be made useful to the officers and soldiers was taken by them during the four days that the troops of the United States remained there. - Pickets, fences, and sugar cane were used as fuel. - On the 28th of December the picket guard which occupied his house was driven in by the Enemy. - On their retreat on the 19th of January a quantity of sugar was still left in his Sugar House, and a great part of his household furniture and other effects still remained in his house -- and both were taken by our Army. -It is impossible in the state of confusion and depredation incident to warfare to ascertain precisely how much injury was done by the enemy and how much destroyed by our troops. - Numerous witnesses who visited his plantation after the evacuation of it by the enemy on the 19th of January 1815 (give) conclusive proof that most of the property contained in his house was left there by the enemy, and that the principal damage was done on that day. Indeed it is not to be presumed that the Enemy under the circumstances of their defeat and hasty retreat would encumber themselves with any but articles of the first necessity, and consequently not merely one half of his loss --- but nearly the whole of it may fairly be attributed to the conduct of the American Army.

Also presented was a sort of inventory entitled "Memorandum of the losses sustained by Col. P. D. Laronde on his Plantation by the American army on the night of the 23rd Decemb'r and morning of 24th, and by a division of about eight hun-

The de La Ronde mansion from a sketch made by Benson J. Lossing in April, 1861. The oak trees forming the avenue are small in size as of that date.

dred mounted men & Dragoons until 28th, when it was taken possession of by the British who held it until 18 Jan'y when they retreated and was again taken possession by our Army."

Among items listed in the inventory were "66 arpens of cane plant burned for want of fuel by order of Col'l Hines and General Coffee. . . . $7290; 40,000 lb. Sugar in 14 hds (hogsheads) destroyed and taken away by our & the Enemy's troops, . . . $ 11,200." Also listed were fence pickets, corn, potatoes and beans, 5 hay carts, 800 bottles of Madeira, and French wines valued at $925, a demijohn of honey and 15 earthen pots of different sizes with sweet meats. There were lists of earthen and glass ware, bedding, furniture, and personal clothing including "25 robes for my wife & daughters - $ 125." De La Ronde had possibly been preparing to have the house re-decorated for. he listed "at cost - Paper hangings for 8 rooms - $244." There were "2 clocks broken to pieces," 2 shades with plated stands & candle sticks, 2 handsome stands plated in bronze for 3 flambeaux, 1 book case, 2 marble tables with Mahogany frames, 1 pr. Mahogany card tables, 1 Toilette Table, 2 dining tables, 4 doz. chairs and among "General articles broken" were "12 beautiful engravings in guilt (sic) frames & a quantity of medicine." Cattle and poultry also were lost as well as powder, shot and fowling pieces, carpentry and cabinet making tools, agricultural utensils, carriages, harness, saddles, etc. Also lost was a library of nearly 400 volumes including works of Voltaire and Racine, and eight slaves, valued at $7.200 were missing.

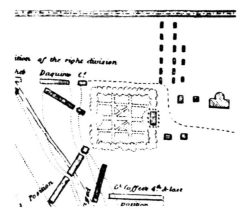

Plan of the gardens and buildings of de La Ronde's plantation at the time of the engagement of December 23, 1814, from Latour's map. The formal garden is surrounded by a hedge of orange trees. The large building with the semi-circular wing in the rear, is the sugar house.

The list is concluded with "Damages done my out houses & dwelling house, sugar and corn mill, &s. . . . $794.20."

This statement was sworn to on June 12, 1815, de La Ronde stating "that to the best of his knowledge and recollection, the above is a true statement of the property lost by him on his plantation by the American and British Armies having alternately possession thereof, from the night of the 23rd of December until the 20th of January last past, when he placed a man on the ground to take care of what was left him."

His friends J. B. Gilly and James Johnston verified the statement, and his neighbors, Fierville and Marcel Bienvenu, attested to the correctness of the sugar estimate. The total claim was for over $40,000.

The name Versailles, so often applied to the place, seems never to have been used during the period of the de La Ronde ownership. De La Ronde died December 1, 1824, and his widow survived him until 1832. Upon her death, it was decided by the numerous heirs that the plantation should be sold at public auction on March 20, 1832. In the advertisements the plantation was described as one of the most valuable in Louisiana:

> The edifices standing on the premises consist of a two story brick house, divided into sixteen rooms — a brick sugar house, containing a very complete Steam Engine imported from England, one Mill, Curing House, forty negro cabins, and all other out buildings required for an extensive establishment.

At the auction, Daniel Warburg was the highest bidder, and acquired the property for $127,000. Warburg was not a planter, but a real estate speculator whose object in making the purchase was revealed a few months later when another advertisement appeared in the local newspapers, announcing: "Sale of De la Ronde's Plantation — to be named Versailles'."

It was Warburg, then, who applied the name Versailles, not to the plantation, but to the subdivision which he made of it in 1832. After describing the location and advantages of the lots, Warburg's advertisement adds that "It is unnecessary to remark that persons wishing to secure country seats by locating on this spot of ground, will not have the inconvenience of the sun in coming to town in the morning and returning in the evening."

The arrangement of Warburg's subdivision appears on Zimpel's map. Paris Road does not appear here. Instead, a canal flanked by de La Ronde and Lake Borgne avenues runs through the middle of the property, "the canal of Versailles intended to communication from the river to the

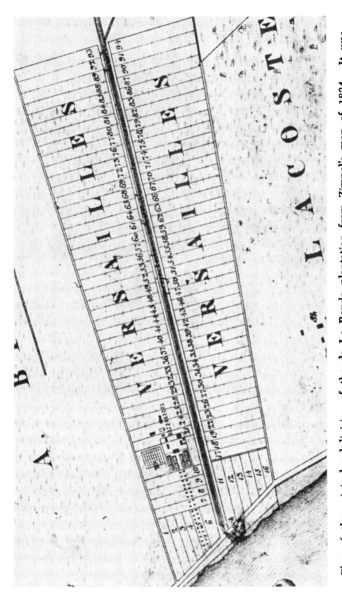

Plan of the original subdivision of the de La Ronde plantation from Zimpel's map of 1834. It was this subdivision to which the name "Versailles" was first applied in 1832.

beautiful Bayou Bienvenu, which empties itself into Lake Borgne.''

The sale advertised in 1832 does not appear to have been too successful. A new scheme of subdivision was then decided upon and the whole tract was laid out in city blocks according to a plan drawn by Joseph Pilié, engineer, on April 10, 1837. This enormous plan, over 20 feet long and somewhat mutilated, is preserved in the Orleans Parish Notarial Archives. It was on this plan that the *Chemin de Paris* or Paris Road first appears. Daniel Warburg sold three blocks to Louis Firmin Caboche on October 27, 1838, which included ''the master house and the other buildings and improvements,'' for $33,000.

Caboche took over the de La Ronde house to establish a college, which he called the College of Versailles. Unfortunately, he was soon in financial difficulties and his creditors took over all his property in 1840, including ''the buildings, and improvements made at Versailles College and the balance of the lease of said Versailles'' to be sold for cash.

The house was later occupied by Louis Janin who bought many of the surrounding blocks which had been sold to various persons, finally restoring the place as a plantation. Following the Civil War, however, like so many of the Louisiana plantations, this one felt hard times and the fine old house suffered neglect and decay, in its last days the ground. floor being used to shelter cattle. Fortunately, a fine photograph was made by Mugnier, the remarkable photographer who in the eighties and nineties made an invaluable rec-

72

Pierre Denis de La Ronde, from Lossing's "Pictorial Field Book of the War of 1812."

ord of many of the old buildings of New Orleans which have now vanished. The negative of this picture, once owned by photographer Dan Leyrer, is labeled "Old Spanish House on the Battlefield of New Orleans." There is no doubt but that this is the de La Ronde house for many of the unique architectural features shown in the picture are still discernible in the ruins. Another valuable relic of the old house is a number of rolls of painted wallpaper, pastoral scenes in rich color which once hung on the walls of the principal rooms. These rolls of paper were presented to the Tulane University Library by a direct descendant of de La Ronde, the late Marie de Hoa Le Blanc of New Orleans.

The house itself burned about 1885, but for many years most of the walls remained standing until

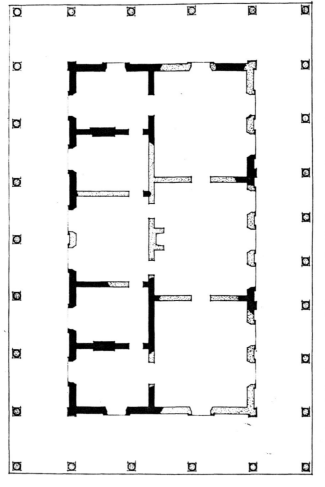

Ground floor plan of the de La Ronde house. The black areas indicate substantial ruins remaining at the time of this reconstruction of the plan was made by the author in 1949.

74

finally blown down by the hurricane of 1915. From what then remained it was possible to reconstruct the plan as shown in the accompanying drawing.

Apart from any consideration of historical association, a study of the ruins immediately discloses the fact that this was a house of the first importance in the history of Louisiana architecture. It was large for a French plantation house, being over 78 feet in breadth and 42 in depth, not including the wide columned galleries with which it was surrounded and of which no traces remain. The plan is most rigidly formal, symmetrical about the center, three principal rooms across the front, facing the river, and five minor ones in the rear. The arrangement is characteristically French of the mid-eighteenth century, and the proportion of the depths of the front and rear rooms is remarkably similar to the proportion found in the plan of the Ursuline Convent on Chartres Street in New Orleans, designed by Ignace François Broutin in 1745. There are other striking similarities between these two plans, including the proportions of the rooms and the fenestration, as well as the treatment of openings with splayed jambs on the interior and broad architraves surrounding them on the exterior. The convent building has rusticated quoins to strengthen the corners and to emphasize the central bay, while the de La Ronde house makes similar use of pilasters. Both building have strong horizontal emphasis in belt courses at the second floor and cornice lines.

Another unusual feature of the house, revealed in the ruins, is the difference in the size of the bricks in the first and second floor walls. Indeed, it is unusual to find the second floor walls of any

Louisiana house of the late eighteenth or early nineteenth century of full masonry. The usual practice was to do the ground floor walls of solid masonry and those of the second floor in colombage, the term locally applied to construction using a heavy wood frame filled in with four or eight inches of brick. The Ursuline Convent was one of the last buidings erected in the French colony where masonry was employed for the walls of both stories.

Although the similarities in the plans of the de La Ronde house and the Ursuline Convent are apparent, they are not as striking as the parallel between this house and another building of Broutin's design, the projected Intendance, the plans for which are dated August 23, 1749.

Family tradition maintains that de La Ronde built his house about the year 1805. What possible connection can it have then with these plans of over half a century earlier? Some connection may lie in the fact that de La Ronde was a grandson of the architect Broutin and may have come into possession of some of his plans. Broutin's daughter, Madeleine, widow of de Lino de Chalmet, married Pierre Denis de La Ronde about 1757, and her son, the supposed builder of the house, was born April 20, 1762, nearly eleven years after Broutin's death, August 9, 1751.

Another curious coincidence is the similarity in plan of this house and the house built about 1750 by Balthazar de Mazan. From the description contained in an inventory made in 1763 at the time it was sold to Louis Boré, it is apparent that the plans must have been almost alike.

Could this be the house whose ruins are still standing? Undoubtedly, it was still standing when de La Ronde bought the place in 1799. De La Ronde may have, however, been influenced by the earlier house in the design of his new one, and may even have incorporated some of its finer features.

The de La Ronde plantation has been a most important one from the very beginning of the French Colony. The original eight arpent tract was granted to a man named Saubugne. He soon gave up the property and it was granted to Adrien de Pauger, then engineer-in-chief of Louisiana who as assistant to Le Blond de la Tour had laid out the original plan of New Orleans in 1721. This grant was probably in compensation for the work he had done since 1721 on a plantation directly across the river from town and from which he was evicted in 1724 by Bienville who claimed it as his own and who then gave it to the Company of the Indies, it later becoming known as the "King's Plantation." Litigation between Pauger and Bienville continued even after the death of the former in 1726. In his will he left his plantation at Point Saint Antoine to the Sieurs Dreux.

The Dreux brothers soon after sold it to a man named Jory Gibery, called St. Martin, and this eight arpents is listed as belonging to him in the Census list of about 1730. It was from him that Mazan bought the plantation upon which he built his great house.

Balthazar de Ponfrac, Sieur de Mazan, had arrived in Louisiana in 1736, a 21 year old cadet "of a very ancient house of Provence," son of "the Noble Louis de Mazan, Captain of His Majesty's galleys in the port of Marseilles."

In 1753 Mazan was promoted to a captaincy in the Marine Troops on the recommendations of Governors Vaudreuil and Kerlerec, and the following year he was permitted to retire because of his poor health and with the added distinction of the award of the Cross of St. Louis and its title of Chevalier.

After his retirement the really significant events of Mazan's career occurred. He evidently managed his affairs well for he had soon built a fine house on his plantation and was regarded as one of the wealthiest men in the colony. At this time interest first began to be shown in the cultivation of sugar in Louisiana. As early as 1742 a few sugar cane plants were being grown by the Jesuits without much success, however, until about 1757 when Claude Joseph Villars Dureuil undertook to begin sugar cane growing on a grand scale. His plantation was located facing the river just below the town, a plantation later to be owned by Bernard de Marigny and to be subdivided into lots as the Faubourg Marigny. Unfortunately, Dubreuil died in November of 1757 but the cultivation of sugar was carried on by Mazan who purchased many of Dubreuil's slaves and equipment when the estate was sold at auction.

Mazan's health did not improve and he finally decided to return to France. He therefore sold his plantation to the Sieur Louis Boré in September 1763. Boré was the father of Jean Etienne Boré who is generally credited with being the founder of the sugar industry in Louisiana. Mazan and Boré were possibly married to sisters, Mazan having married a Marie Carriere and Boré, a Celeste Therese Carriere. Boré moved into the

Ruins of the de La Ronde mansion from a photograph made by the late Stanley Clisby Arthur before large sections of the walls were blown down by the hurricane of 1915.

plantation house and continued the cultivation of sugar while Mazan took up his residence in his town house on Royal Street, before journeying to France.

On his return to Louisiana, Mazan became involved in the Revolution of 1768, against Spanish rule in Louisiana.

Upon his conviction and sentencing to ten years in prison, all his properties were forfeited to the Spanish Crown and the old planter spent his declining years in prison. He was eventually pardoned.

On January 23, 1770, the confiscated plantation was sold at auction by order of Governor O'Reilly, and purchased for ten thousand pounds by Don Bartolomé Macnemara, a militia captain. A survey to confirm his title was made on December 12, 1771, by Don Luis Andry and shows the principal house far back from the river, opposite the point where the plantation widens out behind part of the Ursuline property. Comparing this with the Zimpel plan engraved in 1834, it would appear that this great Mazan house was located on lots 83 and 88 nearly at the back of the Versailles subdivision while the de La Ronde house on Lot 20 was near the front, indicating rather conclusively that these were two distinct and different houses.

Macnemara sold the plantation to Doña Francisca Macarty, widow of Le Breton who the following year married Maurice Conway. Upon her death in 1787 Conway became sole owner and in April, 1789, sold it to Jean Baptiste Dartigaux, making a settlement of their mother's estate the following year with his stepchildren, Barthelemy

Le Breton and Jeanne Françoise Le Breton, wife of Joseph Xavier de Pontalba.

In May of 1791 Dartigaux sold the property to his father-in-law, Joseph Connand, who died in 1798. At his succession sale on February 13, 1799, Pierre Denis de La Ronde became the owner. In February, 1801, he increased his river frontage by the purchase of four arpents of the former Ursuline plantation from Pierre Lacoste, the four arpents acquired by him from Joseph Soniat Dufossat whose father, Guy Soniat Dufossat, had bought the twenty arpent plantation from the Ursulines in 1778.

The de La Ronde house must have been the finest house of its period in Louisiana and, considering the important part it played in the Battle of New Orleans, and the importance of the plantation in colonial days, it should be restored. Enough is left in the ruins so that, with other photographic and documentary evidence available, it would be possible to authentically reconstruct this great house and restore its splendid avenue of oaks as one of the outstanding historic shrines in the country.

VIII. THE LACOSTE PLANTATION

Continuing down the river beyond de La Ronde, the next plantation at the time of the Battle of New Orleans was that of Pierre Robin Lacoste. The old house that was pointed out as Lacoste's was still standing about 1950, but has now disappeared. It was a typical Louisiana plantation house raised on a brick basement, surrounded by galleries, and covered with a generous hipped roof that extended over them to protect them and

Lacoste's Mansion from Benson J. Lossing's "Pictorial Field Book of the War of 1812" probably from a sketch made in 1861.

also the walls of the house from sun and rain. An unusual feature of the house was that the brick walls of the basement actually consisted of a series of large brick arches.

When the writer visited the house a few years before its demolition, it was extremely delapidated and in the last stages of decay. The old brick arches of the basement seemed to be of undoubted antiquity, perhaps dating back to the Spanish Colonial Period, but the upper part of the house appeared to have been rebuilt in a late Victorian manner. Perhaps the old house had burned or been so extensively remodeled that no details of an early period could be recognized. In mass and form, however, the house still retained something of its original character.

Like most of the plantations along the river,

this one can be traced back almost to the time of the founding of New Orleans in 1718. On one of the earliest maps of these plantations, the one probably made by Pauger in 1723, part of this property is shown as belonging "to M. Davion of the Seminary." This was Father Davion who was sent out as a missionary by the Seminary of Quebec in 1698 and became one of the most noted missionaries in the early years of French exploration and colonization in the Mississippi Valley.

Upon his departure from Louisiana in 1725 and his death in France in 1726, Father Davion's plantation probably reverted to the Company of the Indies, and so, to fulfill the obligation of providing a plantation for raising cattle and provisions for the newly arrived Ursulines, it was granted to them. Sister Madeleine Hachard, in a letter to her father on October 27, 1727, shortly after her arrival in New Orleans, said that the Company had provided several slaves, to cultivate their property. "This plantation is only a league from here," the nun wrote. "We have a manager and his wife there who take care of our interests."

The Ursulines retained ownership of this plantation, which they ultimately enlarged to 20 arpents, until 1778, when, planning to buy another and smaller plantation uptown near what is still known as Religious Street, they sold the plantation to Guy Soniat Dufossat. A plan of the plantation, dated June 1, 1803, shows only one property, Soignac (Soniat), between La Ronde and Jumonville. This was the property that subsequently became the Lacoste and Villere plantations.

On June 27, 1730, according to a contract at the Cabildo, a builder by the name of Michael Vien agreed to build on this plantation for Raymond Amyault, Esquire, Sieur D'Ausseville "a house forty five to fifty feet long by twenty two feet or more wide, as the length of the wood will permit. The said building shall have two frame cross walls which will form three chambers; twelve windows; and a gallery five feet wide all around. The said house (shall be) on sills, well framed and with St. Andrew croses in all the voids, and erected upon blocks four to five feet high, the rafters strong and set close enough together in order to be roofed with double planks in the Canadian manner. . . . There will be paid to me after the said house is done, the sum of two hundred fifty livres."

This house was typical of the plantation houses of the French Colonial period. It probably passed into possession of the Ursulines and was sold with their original eight arpent grant, to Guy Soniat Dufossat, with the principal house and the rest of the buildings with the exception of the pits or vats for the manufacture of indigo which belonged to a Don Joseph Gallien. The property was described as being a league and a half below New Orleans.

On February 12, 1794, some years after purchasing the plantation from the Ursulines, Dufossat sold part of it — the upper four arpents, sixty arpents in depth — to his son, Joseph Soniat Dufossat.

Guy Soniat Dufossat died soon afterwards and the plantation was inherited by his widow, the former Claudina Dreux. On February 1, 1796, before the notary, Pedro Pedesclaux, her son, Joseph, sold the four arpents he had bought from his father, to Pierre Lacoste, and five years later, on February 1, 1801, Lacoste sold it to his neighbor, Pierre Denis de La Ronde. It is interesting to note that Lacoste's wife was Doña Pelagia Dreux, perhaps the same family as the Widow Dufossat.

Eventually Pierre Lacoste became owner of the entire sixteen arpents of the former Dufossat plantation, but bought it in three different portions.

The Lacoste plantation played an important part in the events of the Battle of New Orleans. After taking over the Villere house as headquarters, the British proceeded to take over Lacoste's on December 23, 1814. According to Latour, British "outposts had been stationed at different places, in an oblique line, extending from the boundary between La Ronde's and Lacoste's plantations, running along the negro huts of the latter, on the back of the dwelling house, as far as a cluster of live oaks, on Villere's canal near the wood." Here the Americans launched their first attack on December 23 and, Latour continues, "Coffee's division discovered that several parties of the enemy were posted among Lacoste's negro huts. On this the General ordered his men to move forward to the right, to drive the enemy from that portion, which was soon effected."

Latour also relates that "The negro huts of Mr. Lacoste's plantation still exhibit evident proof of the unerring aim of the gallant Tennesseans of Coffee's division: in one spot particularly are seen half a dozen marks of their balls in a diameter of four inches, which were probably all fired at the same object." After the initial encounter on December 23, the Americans withdrew to de La

85

Ronde's plantation, and Lacoste's remained in the hands of the enemy until after the battle of January 8, Major Lacoste himself, meanwhile, rendering gallant service under Jackson, commanding troops of free men of color.

After the British took over Lacoste's plantation, Alexander Dickson wrote on December 26, that "I accompanied Sir Edward to our advance, which is at a plantation about half a mile in front of Head Quarters (Mr. Lacoste's home see plan) . . . Col. Thornton . . . has thrown up works and made his position at Lacoste's house very strong." According to Dickson, General Pakenham slept at Lacoste's house on January 1, and on January 3 Dickson set up a workshop there for repairing gun-carriage. When the British finally withdrew they took with them many of the plantation slaves, but apparently left the house intact.

Zimpel's map of 1834 shows the Lacoste plantation with its principal house located near its lower boundary, the adjacent plantation of G. Villere. Above was the former de La Ronde plantation, shown subdivided as "Versailles," a property widening out toward the rear behind more than half of the Lacoste lands.

In its last years the Lacoste house, in a heavy grove of live oaks, was much farther back from the river than it was in 1815 due to the building up of the batture in this area. When a water purification plant was constructed between the old house and the highway, the St. Bernard Parish water board hoped to spare at least the 15 handsome brick arches. The Board did then invite preservation plans, but the house was too far gone and soon even the ancient arches disappeared.

IX. THE VILLERE PLANTATION

When the invading British Army entered Bayou Bienvenu from Lake Borgne, they followed a route selected for them by their scouts, Captain Spencer and Lieutenant Peddie. Turning off to the left, they entered Bayou Mazant which led up to the rear of the de La Ronde plantation. Low water, however, prevented the barges from continuing on to the de La Ronde canal, so they turned instead into the canal that led to the Villere plantation and, finding solid ground along its banks, landed there and proceeded on toward the river. Thus it happened that the first plantation the British captured was that of Jacques Philippe Villere and his son, Gabriel. This notable plantation became and remained the British headquarters throughout the compaign, rather than the more elegant and spacious de La Ronde house that had been selected by the scouts.

With a number of his men, Major Gabriel Villere was captured in his own house by the first invaders but managed to make a daring escape and spread the alarm. The dramatic story of his leap through the window, across the gallery and over the railing to safety in the trees and swamp, has often been told. For nearly a century the house continued to be an object of the greatest interest to visitors.

The Villere plantation was known as "Conseil" and the master house was a rather simple one story structure raised only a few feet above the ground and surrounded by a gallery. A view of the house that appeared in Lossing's *Pictorial Field Book of the War of 1812* shows it as having a hipped roof with two chimneys rising near the ridge and with dormer windows, all very French in feeling. A note accompanying this illustration states: "This is from a sketch made by the author in April, 1861. The buildings seen in the distance, beyond the avenue of trees, were the sugar works of the plantation." A later photograph of the house made by Stanley Clisby Arthur in the early 1900's shows the house just as it appears in the Lossing sketch except that the dormers are missing and the roof has gable ends instead of hips. Grace King in *Creole Families of New Orleans*, published in 1921, says that "The Villere house exists no longer, having been destroyed by fire, but its substitute, a low cottage with gallery in front, preserves a likeness of the home . . ." Perhaps it was only the roof that was destroyed by fire and was rebuilt in a slightly different form.

Another sketch of this gable-ended house appeared in the *Daily Picayune* on January 18, 1891, with an interesting account of a visit to the house at that time. Besides, this sketch shows the curious two story wing close to the house — a wing only indicated behind the trees in the Lossing sketch. This wing was the last fragment of the historic house to be left standing and was in ruinous condition when last seen by the writer in the 1930's. No trace of the main body of the house then remained but its location could be recognized by the interesting cluster of live oaks planted in the form of a great rectangle in back of the house. Another sketch of the house from the rear appears in Cable's *The Creoles of Louisiana*, published in 1884. Here the great oaks and the two story wing are prominently shown.

"Conseil," plantation home of Jacques Philippe Villere from an old newspaper photograph. The two-story wing to the right was the last part of the house to remain standing.

On Latour's map of Jackson's night attack on December 23, Villere's house is indicated as British General Keane's Headquarters. He indicates a rather small house with a formal garden in front enclosed on the front and lower side by fences and on the other two sides by a hedge of trees, possibly oranges. In the rear, larger buildings for the sugar works are shown and to the left and rear of the house, along the canal, are the negro cabins. Alexander Dickson's sketch shows a somewhat different arrangement of buildings and the garden is not indicated except by a fence. Here the house appears larger and the wing on the lower side is more clearly shown. Dickson also shows several guns set up by the British in front along the levee. Latour adds that "A few pieces of cannon had already arrived, and were mounted in the court near Villere's canal, near the negro huts. General Keane and his officers, among whom was Colonel Thornton, had established their headquarters in Mr. Villere's house."

It was on Christmas Day that General Pakenham arrived at the Villere house and took over command of the British forces. Alexander Dickson, who accompanied him, also slept in a small room at the house which is said "is very full." The next day, however, he moved to a Negro hut.

After the battle of January 8 and the death of General Pakenham, the British continued to occupy Villere's house until January 18 when it was evacuated.

Jacques Philippe Villere was born in Louisiana in 1761 only a few years before his father was killed by the Spanish authorities as a result of his part in the revolution of 1768. Young Villere was educated in France and after the Battle of New Orleans became second Governor of Louisiana, the first Creole to be elected to this office. He died on March 7, 1830; his wife, Jeanne Henriette Fazende, had died August 26, 1826. The plantation, however, remained in the family for many years.

On July 7, 1836, the Villere heirs sold the inherited property to Caliste Villere, one of the brothers. It was then described as:

> A sugar plantation situated in St. Bernard Parish at around seven miles below New Orleans on the left bank of the Mississippi river, known under the name of 'Conseil Plantation,' measuring around nineteen arpents front to the said river by a depth extending as far as Lake Borgne (if the titles give this right, the depth of eighty arpents only being guaranteed) and bounded on its upper limit by the Lacoste plantation and on its lower limit by the Cucullu plantation, together with the buildings, circumstances, dependencies, agricultural instruments and tools belonging to the said plantation . . . and forty seven slaves attached to the said plantation.

A mortgage mentioned in an act by the notary, Theodore Seghers, in 1837 indicates that Gabriel Villere was then the owner of "Conseil."

He is shown on Zimpel's map of 1834 as the owner, with the house with its great rectangle of oaks in the rear shown located above the canal and the boundary of the adjacent plantation belonging to the "Succession of S. Cucullu." This part of the property, consisting of about 7¼ arpents had been purchased by Jacques Villere and his son Gabriel from Bernard Marigny on July 2, 1808. Jacques Villere already owned the upper part of the property adjoining Lacoste, but no buildings are shown on it on Zimpel's map.

91

Marigny actually owned the property for only three days. He had purchased it on June 30, 1808, from Joseph Soniat Dufossat, accepting it in partial payment for a plantation about four leagues above the city.

Following the Louisiana Purchase in 1803, when plantation owners sought to have the titles to their land confirmed, Jacques Villere applied for confirmation of a tract of a little more than five arpents, bounded above by Norbert Boudousquie and below by Soniat Dufossat. At the same time Boudousquie was confirmed in his title to about five arpents, bounded above by Doriocourt and below by Villere. Villere later obtained the Boudousquie tract resulting, with the 7¼ arpents he purchased from Soniat Dufossat, in the 19 of so arpents he left to his heirs.

According to the 1803 map of the river plantations only the Soniat plantation existed between de La Ronde and Jumonville, the area that in 1815 was both the Villere and Lacoste properties. The French map of 1753 shows a plantation belonging to Dalbi (Darby) immediately below the Ursuline Nuns plantation.

It is particularly interesting to note that both the Lacoste and Villere plantations that served as British headquarters in 1814-15 had, for so many years in the French and Spanish Colonial periods, belonged to an English gentleman, Jonathas Darby, who must have been one of the very few Englishmen in the colony at such an early date.

X. THE JUMONVILLE PLANTATION

The last plantation on the East Bank of the river below New Orleans to be directly involved in the events of the battles of 1814-15 was that of Charles Coulon Jumonville de Villiers. This was the house of one of the oldest and most distinguished French-Canadian families in Louisiana.

Charles Coulon Jumonville de Villiers' plantation fronted nearly 20 arpents along the Mississippi river just below the Villere plantation. When the British took it over as their headquarters, they soon drove the Americans from Jumonville's and took that over, also. According to Latour, "Colonel Denis de La Ronde . . . had stationed detachments of his regiment, the third of Louisiana militia, on . . . Jumonville's plantation . . ." These troops withdrew down river. In the engagement of December 23, 1814, the militia at English Turn under General David Morgan, hearing the gun fire of Jackson's attack farther up, advanced almost as far as Jumonville's bridge where they fired on the enemy, but, fearing an ambush, returned to English Turn.

A few days later, Jackson ordered General Morgan to cut the levee below the enemy, at Jumonville's. Although this operation was promptly and successfully executed under the direction of Major Lafon, the river was too low for this break in the levee at Jumonville's to produce the desired result.

Towards the end of December, Latour reports that "The British . . . hospitals were established in the buildings of Jumonville's plantation, where their black troops were stationed. The British

93

had taken all the horses belonging to the plantations, from Bienvenu's to Jumonville's inclusively . . ."

No description of the buildings of Jumonville's plantation at the time of the battle have been found, but they must have been extensively damaged, for in 1823 he was forced to mortgage the property "because of losses due to the English invasion." Seven years later, on February 9, 1830, he exchanged it with Simon Cucullu for several of Cucullu's many properties in the Vieux Carre.

Attached to this act of exchange is a most complete collection of original documents to support the title, documents that Cucullu was to use to reinforce his claim for confirmation before the Federal Land Office. These documents trace the ownership of Jumonville's plantation in unbroken succession back to a grant by the French Colonial Governor, Etienne de Perier, in 1729.

Jumonville's wife, Aimee Beaumont Enoul Livaudais, gave her consent to the sale in exchange for a house and lot on Bourbon Street, and a lot at the corner of Chartres and Dumaine Streets.

Cucullu did not long enjoy his plantation, for in October, 1833, he died, probably at his city residence, the house now one of the buildings of the Maison Hospitalière at 822 Barracks Street.

In the inventory of Cucullu's estate made by Gustave Le Gardeur on October 15, 1833, the appraisal ends with a most interesting listing of the plantation buildings:

> There is on this plantation a principal house, a hospital, a kitchen, a storehouse, stables, pigeon cotes, negro cabins, as well as several other small buildings; a sugar

house, refinery and mill, the whole in a vast building constructed of bricks, a steam engine, a saw mill and (another) mill operated by the said steam engine, which likewise serves for the fabrication of sugar; a pending crop consisting of twenty five arpents of first (quality) cane and two hundred sixty five arpents of plain, as well as one hundred fifty arpents of corn. The whole estimated at the sum of $80,000.

The plantation had been purchased from Renato de Kernion by Jumonville in 1795.

De Kernion had bought the same plantation on August 22, 1789, from the succession of Charlotte Lalande d'Apremont, widow of Pierre Chabert, who had inherited it from her late husband. The property had been bought by Chabert, a former captain of infantry in the service of France when Louisiana was still under French rule, from the Sieur Gerard Pery and his wife, in 1765.

Two years after his purchase, Chabert had a plan drawn of his plantation by the royal surveyor, Pierre François Olivier DeVezan, assisted by his aide, Olivier de St. Maurice. This very fine drawing is attached to the act of exchange between Jumonville and Cucullu.

The survey shows the arrangement of buildings and fences on this important colonial plantation. A large area near the center facing the river was fenced to enclose the principal buildings. The fence curved in from the front in semi-circular or "horse-shoe" form to the carriage gate. At the rear of the large entrance court was the principal house with the dining room in a separate building beside it. Within the entrance court and flanking the approach to the house were two dove cotes or "pigeonnieres", behind one of which, and forming one side of the entrance court, was a large barn and a bakery, while forming the opposite side, nearer the dining room, was the kitchen and a hospital. To one side of the entrance court behind the barn was a fenced-in poultry yard, while back of the principal house and dining room was another large, almost square, fenced-in area designated as the fruit and vegetable garden. Beyond the fence, on the lower side, a "mill canal" or large ditch led back from the river through the fields, probably to Bayou Mazan. Across this canal and centered on the principal house were three rows of "camps and cabins for the negroes," each row containing seven buildings.

Pery had bought the plantation on September 17, 1740, from the succession of Bertrand Jaffre; called La Liberté, who had died in March of that year having named Pery as executor of his estate. The plantation was, however, apparently bought with Pery's wife's funds, for on August 7, 1755, she had petitioned Monsieur D'Auberville, of the Superior Council, to permit her to sell the property.

When Olivier DeVezin surveyed the plantation for Chabert in 1768 he mentioned that it was based on a concession made on April 22, 1729, to a man named Jaffre "who was then only the second owner of this land."

Thus it can be seen that the Jumonville plantation that figured in the Battle of New Orleans, was, for the most part, the same land that had been granted to Bertrand Jaffre in 1729, and the buildings that the British used for hospital purposes may actually have been some of the same buildings shown on the survey made when it was Chabert's plantation in 1768.

The Louisiana Landmarks Society

The Louisiana Landmarks Society was established in 1950. However, its historic preservation advocacy activities began at the start of 1949 when members of the formative New Orleans chapter of the Society of Architectural Historians (an outgrowth of a history of Louisiana architecture course taught at Tulane University by Samuel Wilson, Jr.) banded together to save an early-nineteenth-century colonial Creole plantation, called the David Olivier House, from demolition. Leading the charge to preserve Gallier Hall in the 1950s and defeat the proposed Riverfront Expressway in the 1960s, Landmarks rapidly defined preservation advocacy in New Orleans. The current mission of the Louisiana Landmarks Society, the city and state's first historic preservation organization, is to promote historic preservation through education, advocacy, and operation of the Pitot House.

The values of the Louisiana Landmarks Society are manifested in the Pitot House, the nonprofit organization's home since 1964. This rare surviving example of colonial-era Creole architecture provides Landmarks with a site for exhibitions and educational programming that promote its preservation message. The historic structure and its interpreted grounds provide a transformative historic house tour experience for local and out-of-town visitors and provide the local public with a historically authentic and aesthetically idyllic setting for private functions.

The Louisiana Landmarks Society's major programs include an annual series of free public lectures on preservation topics, award recognition for outstanding preservation efforts, and the presentation of New Orleans' Nine Most Endangered properties—a program modeled after the National Trust for Historic Preservation's Eleven Most Endangered program.

In 1987, the board of trustees of the Louisiana Landmarks Society established a publication fund, named in honor of Samuel Wilson, Jr. The object of Landmarks' publication activity is to foster a more general interest in the architectural tradition of the region and to encourage publication of regional architectural history research. In the years since, Landmarks has published and marketed numerous monographs on architecture and preservation topics. By 2010, efforts to expand Landmarks' publishing program resulted in the creation of a publishing and distribution partnership with Pelican Publishing Company. Landmarks' share of proceeds from this partnership will support perpetuation of the Samuel Wilson, Jr. Publication Fund and its mission to provide for the development of future Louisiana Landmarks Society publications.

CPSIA information can be obtained at www.ICGtesting.com
Printed in the USA
LVOW091335261111

256558LV00001B/1/P

9 781589 809963